Orton Gillingham Decodable 3rd Grade Readers

Easy decodable texts to improve reading and writing skills in struggling readers and kids with dyslexia

Volume 4

BrainChild

Introduction

Teaching a child with dyslexia to read: Dyslexia is a specific and persistent learning disability that affects reading and writing. For children with dyslexia, learning to read and write can be a difficult challenge for families and educators to tackle. For these children, written language becomes a great barrier, often without meaning or logic, which generates rejection of the task, frustration and discomfort.

The child with dyslexia is a child who has significant difficulties in reading and writing, because their brain processes information differently than other children; which is why if we expect the same results following the traditional method, we will find many barriers that can and often do harm the child. It is important to become aware of the characteristics of this difficulty, so as to help the child learn to read and the consequent overcoming of their difficulties such as understanding, knowledge and attention to their needs.

Reading difficulties with dyslexia

Dyslexia is a learning disability of neurobiological origin, which causes seem to be in the maturation and structuring of certain brain structures.

Dyslexia is therefore a condition of the brain which causes it to process information differently, making it difficult for the person to understand letters, their sounds, their combinations, etc.

Human language is a language based on signs, letters, and their sounds, which are arbitrary. The correspondence of each grapheme (letter) with its phoneme (sound), does not follow any logic; it's simply chance. This is one of the greatest difficulties that children face when they must learn to read and write. Converting the spoken language, they know into signs and transforming sounds into letters is a challenge.

This is even more complicated in children with dyslexia; the relationship becomes something indecipherable for them. No matter how hard they try, they cannot make sense of that dance between letters and sounds. Children with dyslexia have a lot of difficulty recognizing letters; sometimes they mistake letters for others, write them backwards, etc.

Another difficulty they face, is knowing the sound that corresponds to each letter; and things get even more complicated when we combine several letters, and we have to know several sounds.

New words are a challenge for them, and they can forget them easily, so they must work hard to acquire them. Sometimes they read certain words effortlessly, but the next day they completely forget them.

When they write, they omit letters, change their position, forget words in a sentence, etc.

Dyslexia also affects reading comprehension. When they read, they are trying really hard to decipher and understand each word, sometimes even each letter; that is why the meaning of the text gets lost.

Reading comprehension: Activities to help develop it in children.

How to teach a child with dyslexia to read

A child with dyslexia has difficulty learning to read and write, because it is hard for them to recognize letters and know which sound, they correspond to. However, the child can learn to read and write and overcome those difficulties.

Remember that dyslexia is a learning difficulty that does not imply any physical or mental handicap; the child with dyslexia has adequate capacities. To teach a child with dyslexia to read, it is essential to know the nature of their difficulties, understand them and use a teaching method that responds to their needs.

A child with dyslexia

A teaching method to help a child with dyslexia read.

In the first place, it is necessary to assess the child, to know their reading and writing level, the nature and characteristics of their difficulties in order to understand their specific needs. For this, it is advisable to seek a specialist.

Reading favors the development of phonological awareness (which consists of the correspondence of the sound with the letter). To do this, start with simple activities, letter by letter. Even if other children around the same age read full texts, it may be necessary to start working letter by letter. Later, we can continue with the words, phrases and texts. It is about dedicating more time and more detail to the learning process.

Phonological awareness worksheets

Use motivational activities that are engaging. Do not limit the child to just paper and pencil: they can make letters out of play dough, write on sand with their fingers, play catch or games such as hangman, word searches, crossword puzzles, etc.
Don't force them to read or read a lot. Try to have them read on a daily basis, little by little; sometimes a sentence or a paragraph is enough. Help them understand what they read, ask them questions, ask them to read again, etc.

Copyright 2023 - All Rights Reserved

Contents of this book may not be reproduced, duplicated or transmitted without direct written permission from the author. Under no circumstances will any legal responsibility or blame be held against the publisher for any reparation, damages or monetary loss due to information herein, either directly o indirectly.

Legal Notice:

You cannot amend, distribute, sell, use, quote or paraphrase any part of the contents within this book without the consent of the author.

Disclaimer note:

Please note that the information contained within this document serves only for educational and entertainment purposes. No warranties of any kind are expressed or implied. Readers acknowledge that the author is not engaging in the rendering of legal, financial, medical or professional advice.

Table of Contents

Exploring ancient Egypt......................page 1-12

Eco warriors ....page 13-24

The Great Barrier Reef......................page 25-36

The island of volcanoes ....page 37-48

Maggie's adventure...........................page 49-60

Creepy crawlers................................page 61-72

Heritage of Native American.............page 73-84

A trip to the zoo...............................page 85-96

Sports camp.....................................page 97-108

Short stories ....page 109-117

Read the story. Identify and underline all the verbs in the story.

Exploring ancient Egypt

In the heart of Ancient Egypt, lived the great Pharaohs who ruled over the land with an iron grip. The Pharaohs were powerful rulers, believed to be descendants of the Gods themselves, and were revered by the common people.

But as time passed, the Pharaohs began to fade away, and their legacy became shrouded in mystery. The pyramids they built, the temples they designed, and the treasures they amassed all stood as a testament to their power and might. However, the secrets of their lives remained hidden.

For centuries, scholars and historians have attempted to unravel the mysteries of the Pharaohs. They have scoured the tombs, pored over ancient texts, and studied the hieroglyphs in search of clues about their lives and times.

One such historian was Dr. Sarah Ahmed, an Egyptologist with a passion for uncovering the secrets of the past. She had spent years studying the hieroglyphs and had even learned to read them fluently. But despite her expertise, there were still many secrets of the Pharaohs that eluded her.

One day, while perusing through the archives of the Egyptian Museum, Dr. Ahmed stumbled upon an ancient text which spoke of a lost temple, hidden deep in the desert sands. It was said to hold the answers to many of the mysteries of the Pharaohs.

Determined to uncover the truth, Dr. Ahmed assembled a team of archaeologists and set out on an expedition to find the lost temple. They journeyed deep into the desert, braving the scorching sun and fierce sandstorms.

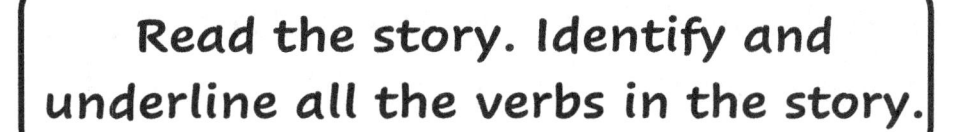

> **Read the story. Identify and underline all the verbs in the story.**

After weeks of searching, they finally stumbled upon an ancient temple, buried deep beneath the sand. As they excavated the site, they uncovered a treasure trove of artifacts, including scrolls, pottery, jewelry, and even mummified remains of the Pharaohs.

As they studied the artifacts, they began to piece together the lives of the Pharaohs. They learned about their customs, their beliefs, and their rituals. They discovered that the Pharaohs were not just rulers, but also spiritual leaders who were worshipped as gods.

Dr. Ahmed even found evidence of a lost Pharaoh, whose name had been erased from history books by his successors. She was able to piece together his story and shed light on his reign, which had been forgotten for centuries.

The discoveries made by Dr. Ahmed and her team were groundbreaking and helped to unravel many of the mysteries of the Pharaohs. Their research shed light on the lives of these ancient rulers and gave us insights into the civilization they built.

Today, we continue to study and learn from the Pharaohs, and their legacy lives on in the magnificent structures they left behind. And thanks to the tireless efforts of historians like Dr. Ahmed, we are able to unearth the secrets of the past and unlock the mysteries of ancient Egypt.

> **Read the story and fill in the blank spaces with the appropriate words.**

Exploring ancient Egypt

- In the heart of Ancient Egypt, lived the great _____ who ruled over the land with an iron grip.
- The Pharaohs were powerful rulers, believed to be descendants of the _____ themselves, and were revered by the common people.
- But as time passed, the Pharaohs began to _____ away, and their legacy became shrouded in mystery.
- The _____ they built, the _____ they designed, and the treasures they amassed all stood as a testament to their power and might.
- However, the _____ of their lives remained hidden.
- For centuries, _____ and historians have attempted to unravel the mysteries of the Pharaohs.
- They have scoured the tombs, pored over ancient texts, and studied the _____ in search of clues about their lives and times.
- One such historian was _____, an Egyptologist with a passion for uncovering the secrets of the past.
- She had spent years studying the _____ and had even learned to read them fluently.
- But despite her expertise, there were still many _____ of the Pharaohs that eluded her.
- One day, while perusing through the archives of the Egyptian Museum, Dr. Ahmed stumbled upon an ancient text which spoke of a lost _____, hidden deep in the desert sands.
- It was said to hold the answers to many of the _____ of the Pharaohs.

Read the story and circle whether the statement is true or false. If the statement is false, provide the correct answer for it.

The Pharaohs were powerful rulers who ruled over Ancient Egypt with an iron grip.

True   False

_____
_____

The Pharaohs were believed to be descendants of the Gods themselves and were revered by the common people.

True   False

_____
_____
_____

The secrets of the lives of the Pharaohs have been fully uncovered and understood by historians.

True   False

_____
_____
_____

Dr. Sarah Ahmed was an archaeologist who was passionate about uncovering the secrets of the past.

True   False

_____
_____

Dr. Ahmed found an ancient text which spoke of a lost temple, hidden deep in the desert sands.

True   False

_____
_____

Read the story 'Exploring ancient Egypt' and answer the following questions.

Who were the Pharaohs and how did they rule over Ancient Egypt?
_____
_____
_____
_____

What was the legacy of the Pharaohs and what mysteries have historians been trying to unravel about their lives?
_____
_____
_____
_____

How did Dr. Sarah Ahmed discover the lost temple and what did her team find there?
_____
_____
_____
_____
_____
_____

What insights did Dr. Ahmed's discoveries provide about the customs, beliefs, and rituals of the Pharaohs?
_____
_____
_____
_____
_____
_____

Why is the study of the Pharaohs and Ancient Egypt important for our understanding of human history and civilization?
_____
_____

Assess your reading fluency by writing the number of words read per minute.

In the heart of Ancient Egypt, lived the great Pharaohs who ruled over the land with an iron grip.	19
The Pharaohs were powerful rulers, believed to be descendants of the God themselves, and were revered by the common people.	39
But as time passed, the Pharaohs began to fade away, and their legacy became shrouded in mystery.	56
The pyramids they built, the temples they designed, and the treasures they amassed all stood as a testament to their power and might.	73
However, the secrets of their lives remained hidden.	87
For centuries, scholars and historians have attempted to unravel the mysteries of the Pharaohs.	101
They have scoured the tombs, pored over ancient texts, and studied the hieroglyphs in search of clues about their lives and times.	123
One such historian was Dr. Sarah Ahmed, an Egyptologist with a passion for uncovering the secrets of the past.	142
She had spent years studying the hieroglyphs and had even learned to read them fluently.	157
But despite her expertise, there were still many secrets of the Pharaohs that eluded her.	172
One day, while perusing through the archives of the Egyptian Museum, Dr. Ahmed stumbled upon an ancient text which spoke of a lost temple, hidden deep in the desert sands.	202
It was said to hold the answers to many of the mysteries of the Pharaohs.	217
Determined to uncover the truth, Dr. Ahmed assembled a team of archaeologists and set out on an expedition to find the lost temple.	240
They journeyed deep into the desert, braving the scorching sun and fierce sandstorms.	253

After weeks of searching, they finally stumbled upon an ancient temple, buried deep beneath the sand.	269
As they excavated the site, they uncovered a treasure trove of artifacts, including scrolls, pottery, jewelry, and even mummified remains of the Pharaohs.	292
As they studied the artifacts, they began to piece together the lives of the Pharaohs.	307
They discovered that the Pharaohs were not just rulers, but also spiritual leaders who were worshipped as gods.	325
Dr. Ahmed even found evidence of a lost Pharaoh, whose name had been erased from history books by his successors.	345
She was able to piece together his story and shed light on his reign, which had been forgotten for centuries.	365
The discoveries made by Dr. Ahmed and her team were groundbreaking and helped to unravel many of the mysteries of the Pharaohs.	387
Their research shed light on the lives of these ancient rulers and gave us insights into the civilization they built.	407
Today, we continue to study and learn from the Pharaohs, and their legacy lives on in the magnificent structures they left behind.	429
And thanks to the tireless efforts of historians like Dr. Ahmed, we are able to unearth the secrets of the past and unlock the mysteries of ancient Egypt.	457

Date			
Words per minute			
Number of errors			

> **Make sentences using the words written below.**

Egypt

Ancient

Explore

Artifacts

History

Expertise

Make a story using only five verbs from the following.

lived   ruled   believed   shrouded
built   fade   designed   stood   studded

> **Read the following story and underline all the adjectives. Use any five adjectives from the paragraph to write a story in your own words.**

Ancient Egypt was a land of wonder, mystery, and breathtaking beauty. Its landscape was characterized by lush greenery, majestic pyramids, and the mighty Nile River. The society was vibrant, colorful, and full of life. The architecture was grand, intricate, and awe-inspiring, with towering columns and ornate carvings. The art was vivid, vibrant, and exquisitely detailed, showcasing the talents of skilled craftsmen. The culture was rich, diverse, and steeped in tradition, with elaborate rituals and customs that celebrated life and the afterlife.

Story

Read the following story and underline all the adverbs. Use any five adverbs from the paragraph to write a story in your own words.

Ancient Egypt was a marvelously advanced civilization that flourished along the banks of the Nile River. Its people lived peacefully and harmoniously, relying greatly on agriculture. They ingeniously developed various techniques in irrigation and farming that allowed them to thrive in the arid desert climate. Their society was highly organized, with individuals fulfilling their specific roles efficiently. They skillfully crafted intricate and awe-inspiring architecture, including pyramids and temples, using quarried stone. Their art was masterfully created and vividly depicted stories of everyday life, religion, and politics. The Egyptians worshipped their gods fervently, building magnificent temples and conducting elaborate rituals. To sum up, Ancient Egypt was an incredibly innovative and fascinating civilization that continues to inspire and amaze us today.

Story

Find and circle the words written below.

Egypt   ancient   history
explore   gods   culture
mystery

a	n	c	i	e	n	t	l	t	h	y	h
e	s	g	c	u	l	t	u	r	e	m	i
s	t	h	o	i	m	p	a	n	z	e	s
e	e	p	i	d	p	e	p	v	e	y	t
r	r	a	n	d	s	a	t	h	e	r	o
o	n	r	p	a	n	e	g	e	e	e	r
l	a	l	e	e	p	g	q	e	e	t	y
p	l	s	j	l	u	y	n	c	r	s	d
x	n	c	e	s	t	p	r	s	t	y	a
e	c	j	b	n	d	t	o	t	h	m	r

> **Read the story. Identify and underline all the nouns in the story.**

Eco Warriors

The Eco Warriors were a group of people who dedicated their lives to protecting the natural world. They were a diverse group, made up of scientists, activists, and everyday citizens who felt a deep connection to the planet.

Their mission was simple: to fight against corporations and governments that threatened the Earth's most precious treasures. They did this through peaceful protests, lobbying, and community outreach programs.

One day, the Eco Warriors received word that a mining company was planning to blast open a mountain in the Amazon rainforest to extract valuable minerals. If they succeeded in their plan, it would destroy not only the mountain but also the surrounding ecosystem and Indigenous communities. The Eco Warriors knew they had to act fast to prevent this from happening.

They organized a march through the streets of the nearest city, calling on people to join them in their fight. As they marched, they chanted slogans and held up signs that read "Protect Our Earth" and "Nature is Not for Sale."

The media took notice of their protest, and soon their message was spreading across the world. They gained support from environmental groups, celebrities, and politicians who shared their passion for protecting the planet.

The Eco Warriors knew they needed more than just protests to stop the mining company. They started legal proceedings and invited lawyers to join their cause. They also reached out to the local Indigenous tribes, who had lived in harmony with the forest for generations. They shared

> **Read the story. Identify and underline all the nouns in the story.**

their knowledge of the land and its ecosystems, and together they formed a powerful alliance.

As the court case dragged on, the Eco Warriors continued their protest. They camped out near the mountain, building tree houses and living off the land. They refused to back down, even when faced with threats from the mining company's security forces.

Finally, after months of legal battles and protests, the court ruled in favor of the Eco Warriors. The mining company was prohibited from blasting open the mountain, and the area was designated a protected zone.

The Eco Warriors celebrated their victory, knowing that their hard work had paid off. They continued their work, protecting nature's treasures wherever they were threatened. They knew that the fight was far from over, and that there would always be new battles to fight.

But they also knew that with each victory, they were one step closer to the world they wanted to see, a world where nature's treasures were valued and protected for generations to come.

Read the story and fill in the blank spaces with the appropriate words.

Eco Warriors

- The Eco Warriors were a group of people who dedicated their lives to protecting the _____ world.
- They were a diverse group, made up of _____, _____, and everyday _____ who felt a deep connection to the planet.
- Their mission was simple: to fight against _____ and governments that threatened the Earth's most precious treasures.
- They did this through peaceful _____, lobbying, and community outreach programs.
- One day, the Eco Warriors received word that a mining company was planning to _____ open a mountain in the Amazon rainforest to extract valuable minerals.
- If they succeeded in their plan, it would destroy not only the mountain but also the surrounding _____ and Indigenous communities.
- The Eco Warriors knew they had to act fast to _____ this from happening.
- They organized a _____ through the streets of the nearest city, calling on people to join them in their fight.
- As they marched, they chanted slogans and held up signs that read "_____" and "Nature is Not for Sale."
- The _____ took notice of their protest, and soon their message was spreading across the world.
- They gained support from _____ groups, celebrities, and politicians who shared their passion for protecting the planet.

> **Read the story and circle whether the statement is true or false. If the statement is false, provide the correct answer for it.**

The Eco Warriors were a group of people who dedicated their lives to protecting the natural world.

True   False

_____
_____
_____

The Eco Warriors were only made up of scientists.

True   False

_____
_____

The mining company planned to extract valuable minerals from a mountain in the Amazon Rainforest.

True   False

_____
_____
_____

The Eco Warriors organized a march through the forest to protest against the mining company.

True   False

_____
_____
_____

The Eco Warriors gained support from environmental groups, celebrities, and politicians who shared their passion for protecting the planet.

True   False

_____
_____

Read the story 'Eco Warriors' and answer the following questions.

Who were the Eco Warriors and what was their mission?

What was the mining company planning to do in the Amazon Rainforest, and why was it a threat to the ecosystem and Indigenous communities?

What other tactics did the Eco Warriors use, besides protests, to try to stop the mining company?

How did the Eco Warriors organize a successful protest against the mining company?

What was the outcome of the court case, and how did the Eco Warriors celebrate their victory?

Assess your reading fluency by writing the number of words read per minute.

The Eco Warriors were a group of people who dedicated their lives to protecting the natural world.	17
They were a diverse group, made up of scientists, activists, and everyday citizens who felt a deep connection to the planet.	38
Their mission was simple: to fight against corporations and governments that threatened the Earth's most precious treasures.	55
They did this through peaceful protests, lobbying, and community outreach programs.	66
One day, the Eco Warriors received word that a mining company was planning to blast open a mountain in the Amazon rainforest to extract valuable minerals.	92
If they succeeded in their plan, it would destroy not only the mountain but also the surrounding ecosystem and Indigenous communities.	114
The Eco Warriors knew they had to act fast to prevent this from happening.	127
They organized a march through the streets of the nearest city, calling on people to join them in their fight.	147
As they marched, they chanted slogans and held up signs that read "Protect Our Earth" and "Nature is Not for Sale."	168
The media took notice of their protest, and soon their message was spreading across the world.	185
They gained support from environmental groups, celebrities, and politicians who shared their passion for protecting the planet.	201
The Eco Warriors knew they needed more than just protests to stop the mining company.	216
They started legal proceedings and invited lawyers to join their cause.	227
They also reached out to the local Indigenous tribes, who had lived in harmony with the forest for generations.	246

They shared their knowledge of the land and its ecosystems, and together they formed a powerful alliance.	263
As the court case dragged on, the Eco Warriors continued their protest.	276
They camped out near the mountain, building tree houses and living off the land.	289
They refused to back down, even when faced with threats from the mining company's security forces.	304
Finally, after months of legal battles and protests, the court ruled in favor of the Eco Warriors.	322
The mining company was prohibited from blasting open the mountain, and the area was designated a protected zone.	339
The Eco Warriors celebrated their victory, knowing that their hard work had paid off.	353
They continued their work, protecting nature's treasures wherever they were threatened. They knew that the fight was far from over, and that there would always be new battles to fight.	383
But they also knew that with each victory, they were one step closer to the world they wanted to see, a world where nature's treasures were valued and protected for generations to come.	416

Date			
Words per minute			
Number of errors			

Make sentences using the words written below.

Warriors

Environment

Scientists

Activists

Citizen

Natural

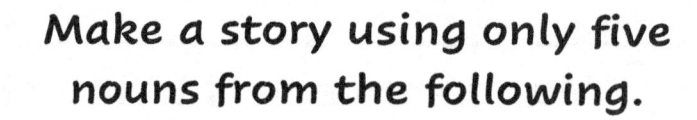

> Make a story using only five nouns from the following.

Eco Warriors   people   lives   natural world   group   scientists   activists   citizens   planet   mission

Read the following paragraph and write the synonyms of the underlined words. Use the underlined words to write a short story.

The Eco Warriors were a group of people who dedicated their lives to protecting the natural world. They were a diverse group, made up of scientists, activists, and everyday citizens who felt a deep connection to the planet.

Their mission was simple: to fight against corporations and governments that threatened the Earth's most precious treasures. They did this through peaceful protests, lobbying, and community outreach programs.

Words	warriors	natural	diverse	deep	mission
Synonyms					

Story

Read the following paragraph and write the synonyms of the underlined words. Use the underlined words to write a short story.

They <u>organized</u> a march through the streets of the <u>nearest</u> city, calling on people to <u>join</u> them in their fight. As they marched, they chanted slogans and held up signs that read "<u>Protect</u> Our Earth" and "Nature is Not for Sale."

The media took notice of their protest, and soon their message was <u>spreading</u> across the world. They gained support from environmental groups, celebrities, and politicians who shared their passion for protecting the planet.

Words	Organized	nearest	protect	spreading	join
Antonyms					

Story

Find and circle the words written below.

activist   eco   warriors
slogans   scientist   citizen

m	c	i	t	i	z	e	n	f	w	h	p
p	s	o	s	c	k	k	q	i	t	e	e
s	n	t	h	i	m	p	a	s	s	e	s
r	u	h	k	g	p	e	p	n	i	m	t
a	c	a	m	e	l	s	j	a	t	n	a
e	r	u	i	t	s	e	g	g	n	a	t
b	r	o	e	k	a	n	s	o	e	e	i
w	c	t	l	a	n	d	s	l	i	c	b
e	w	a	r	r	i	o	r	s	c	o	a
a	c	t	i	v	i	s	t	e	s	t	h

Read the story. Identify and underline all the verbs in the story.

The Great Barrier Reef

The Great Barrier Reef is one of the greatest natural wonders of the world, a vast expanse of coral that stretches over 2,300 kilometers along the eastern coast of Australia. But what many people do not know is the incredible diversity of marine life that thrives beneath the waves.

As you dive into the depths of the reef, you enter a world of unimaginable beauty and wonder. Schools of brightly colored fish dart around you, while sea turtles gracefully glide by. You can see schools of parrotfish, angelfish, and butterflyfish swimming through the coral formations that provide shelter and food for a myriad of sea creatures.

As you continue your descent, you might spot a giant clam, its massive shell providing a home for smaller fish and invertebrates. Or you might come across a cuttlefish, camouflaged against the reef, changing colors to blend in with its surroundings.

But the real marvels of the Great Barrier Reef lie in its larger inhabitants. Giant manta rays, with wingspans of up to 7 meters, glide effortlessly through the water. And then there are the sharks, not to be feared, but to be respected, including the gentle whale shark, the largest fish in the world.

The highlight of any trip to the Great Barrier Reef is undoubtedly the chance to swim with one of the most majestic creatures of the sea: the humpback whale. These gentle giants migrate to the waters of the reef each year, breaching and slapping their tails as they communicate with one another.

Beyond the creatures that can be seen with the naked eye, there are also the ecosystems that exist within the reef. The tiny coral polyps that form the foundation of the reef are home to a vast array of microscopic organisms that help to sustain the entire ecosystem.

> **Read the story. Identify and underline all the nouns in the story.**

Among these organisms are tiny planktonic creatures that drift with the currents, providing food for larger creatures. And then there are the sea grass beds, vast fields of underwater vegetation that provide shelter and food for animals such as dugongs, sea turtles, and a variety of fish.

As you emerge from the depths of the reef and return to the surface, you are left with a sense of awe and wonder at the incredible diversity of life that exists beneath the waves. The Great Barrier Reef is not just a marvel of nature, but a reminder of the interconnectedness of all life on Earth, and the need to protect and preserve our precious natural resources.

Read the story and fill in the blank spaces with the appropriate words.

The Great Barrier Reef

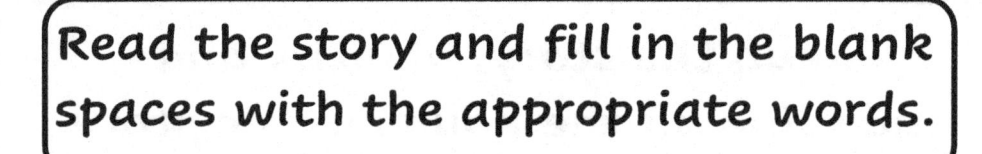

- The Great Barrier Reef is one of the greatest natural wonders of the world, a vast expanse of coral that stretches over _____ kilometers along the eastern coast of Australia.
- But what many people do not know is the incredible diversity of _____ life that thrives beneath the waves.
- As you dive into the depths of the _____, you enter a world of unimaginable beauty and wonder.
- _____ of brightly colored fish dart around you, while sea turtles gracefully glide by.
- You can see schools of _____, angelfish, and butterflyfish swimming through the coral formations that provide shelter and food for a myriad of sea creatures.
- As you continue your descent, you might spot a giant _____, its massive shell providing a home for smaller fish and invertebrates.
- Or you might come across a _____, camouflaged against the reef, changing colors to blend in with its surroundings.
- But the real marvels of the _____ lie in its larger inhabitants.
- Giant _____ rays, with wingspans of up to 7 meters, glide effortlessly through the water.
- And then there are the _____, not to be feared, but to be respected, including the gentle whale shark, the largest fish in the world.
- The highlight of any trip to the Great Barrier Reef is undoubtedly the chance to swim with one of the most majestic creatures of the sea: _____.

Read the story and circle whether the statement is true or false. If the statement is false, provide the correct answer for it.

The Great Barrier Reef is located along the eastern coast of Australia.

True　　　　　　　　False

Marine life does not thrive beneath the waves of the Great Barrier Reef.

True　　　　　　　　False

Schools of brightly colored fish are a common sight in the reef.

True　　　　　　　　False

A giant clam's shell can provide a home for larger sea creatures.

True　　　　　　　　False

Humpback whales migrate to the waters of the reef to communicate with other whales.

True　　　　　　　　False

Sea grass beds do not provide shelter or food for any animals.

True　　　　　　　　False

Read the story 'The Great Barrier Reef' and answer the following questions.

Where is the Great Barrier Reef located, and what makes it a natural wonder of the world?

What kind of marine life can be found beneath the waves of the Great Barrier Reef, and what role do they play in the ecosystem?

What are some examples of the larger creatures that can be seen when diving into the depths of the reef?

How do the tiny coral polyps that make up the foundation of the reef support the entire ecosystem, and what other microscopic organisms exist within the reef?

Assess your reading fluency by writing the number of words read per minute.

The Great Barrier Reef is one of the greatest natural wonders of the world, a vast expanse of coral that stretches over 2,300 kilometers along the eastern coast of Australia.	30
But what many people do not know is the incredible diversity of marine life that thrives beneath the waves.	49
As you dive into the depths of the reef, you enter a world of unimaginable beauty and wonder.	67
As we hiked through the forest, we marveled at the beauty of nature around us.	71
Schools of brightly colored fish dart around you, while sea turtles gracefully glide by.	81
You can see schools of parrotfish, angelfish, and butterflyfish swimming through the coral formations that provide shelter and food for a myriad of sea creatures.	106
As you continue your descent, you might spot a giant clam, its massive shell providing a home for smaller fish and invertebrates.	128
Or you might come across a cuttlefish, camouflaged against the reef, changing colors to blend in with its surroundings.	147
But the real marvels of the Great Barrier Reef lie in its larger inhabitants. Giant manta rays, with wingspans of up to 7 meters, glide effortlessly through the water.	176
And then there are the sharks, not to be feared, but to be respected, including the gentle whale shark, the largest fish in the world.	201
The highlight of any trip to the Great Barrier Reef is undoubtedly the chance to swim with one of the most majestic creatures of the sea: the humpback whale.	230

These gentle giants migrate to the waters of the reef each year, breaching and slapping their tails as they communicate with one another.	253
Beyond the creatures that can be seen with the naked eye, there are also the ecosystems that exist within the reef.	274
The tiny coral polyps that form the foundation of the reef are home to a vast array of microscopic organisms that help to sustain the entire ecosystem.	301
Among these organisms are tiny planktonic creatures that drift with the currents, providing food for larger creatures.	308
And then there are the sea grass beds, vast fields of underwater vegetation that provide shelter and food for animals such as dugongs, sea turtles, and a variety of fish.	348
As you emerge from the depths of the reef and return to the surface, you are left with a sense of awe and wonder at the incredible diversity of life that exists beneath the waves.	383
The Great Barrier Reef is not just a marvel of nature, but a reminder of the interconnectedness of all life on Earth, and the need to protect and preserve our precious natural resources.	416

Date			
Words per minute			
Number of errors			

Make sentences using the words written below.

Coral reef
_____
_____

Ecosystem
_____
_____

Barrier
_____
_____

Backpacks
_____
_____

Nature
_____
_____

Raccoon
_____
_____

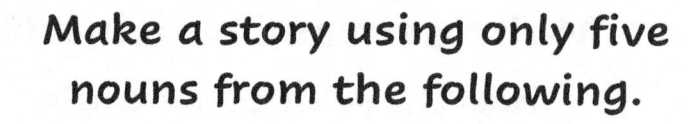

Make a story using only five nouns from the following.

Australia   diversity   marine life   waves
school   fish   sea turtles   parrotfish
angelfish   butterflyfish

Read the following paragraph, identify, and underline all the adjectives. Use the underlined words to write a short story.

The Great Barrier Reef is a magnificent natural wonder that spans over 2,300 kilometers along the eastern coast of Australia. It is an expansive and diverse ecosystem that is home to an incredible array of marine life, from brightly colored fish to gentle giants like the humpback whale. The coral formations are both vibrant and delicate, providing shelter for countless creatures, and the crystal-clear waters offer a glimpse into a world of unimaginable beauty and wonder. Its breathtaking expanse is awe-inspiring, and its fragility reminds us of the need to protect and preserve our planet's natural treasures.

Story

Read the following paragraph and underline all the adverbs. Use the adverbs to make sentences.

The Great Barrier Reef is a spectacularly diverse ecosystem that stretches majestically along the eastern coast of Australia. The brightly colored fish dart around gracefully while the sea turtles swim slowly and steadily. The coral formations provide essential nutrients and shelter for the marine creatures that rely on them heavily. The manta rays glide effortlessly through the water, and the humpback whales migrate purposefully to the reef each year. The reef is an incredibly beautiful and fragile natural wonder that needs to be protected vigilantly. It's awe-inspiringly vast and truly fascinating to explore, but we must view it respectfully and responsibly.

Adverbs	Sentences

Find and circle the words written below.

great barrier reef   coral
aquatic   animals   home
underwater

g	r	e	a	t	r	e	e	f	w	a	b
c	h	a	n	i	m	a	l	s	f	e	a
o	c	c	h	i	m	b	p	i	r	x	r
r	i	h	t	o	p	e	g	l	u	c	r
a	t	l	a	k	m	e	j	l	i	i	i
l	a	r	r	a	b	e	g	e	t	t	e
i	u	e	n	t	s	s	q	h	s	i	r
n	q	o	r	e	s	t	i	s	n	n	v
g	a	y	o	a	m	y	d	s	s	g	d
c	u	n	d	e	r	w	a	t	e	r	a

Read the story. Identify and underline all the nouns in the story.

The island of volcanoes

In the heart of a lush tropical island lived a community of people who had learned to coexist with the warm volcanoes that surrounded their village. Every day, they would wake up to the gentle rumble of the earth beneath their feet and the steam rising from the nearby mountains.

The villagers had always known that life on this island was different from anywhere else. The warm volcanoes provided a natural source of energy that they used to cook their food, heat their homes, and even power their boats. They had also learned how to harness the heat from the volcanoes to help grow their crops and keep their animals warm during the cooler months.

One day, as the villagers were tending to their fields, they noticed something strange happening around the base of one of the volcanoes. The ground was shaking violently, and steam was pouring out of the fissures in the earth. The villagers knew that this could only mean one thing, the volcano was about to erupt.

In a panic, the villagers ran towards the village to warn the others. They gathered in the center of the town, unsure of what to do next. Suddenly, an old man stepped forward. He had lived on the island for many years and had seen his fair share of volcanic eruptions.

"Everyone, calm down", he said. "We have been preparing for this moment for years. We know exactly what to do."

The villagers looked at the old man in disbelief. How could anyone be prepared for something like this?

> **Read the story. Identify and underline all the nouns in the story.**

The old man led the villagers to a large underground cave system that had been carved out around the base of one of the warm volcanoes. Inside, they found a network of tunnels and rooms that had been built to withstand the heat and pressure of an eruption.

As the villagers huddled in the safety of the caves, they watched in awe as the volcano erupted outside. Lava spewed from the top of the mountain, and ash rained down from the sky. But the villagers were safe, protected by the secure walls of the underground caves.

When the eruption had ceased, the villagers emerged from the caves, unscathed and amazed at the power of the warm volcanoes. They knew that they would continue to live in harmony with these natural wonders, using their warmth and energy to sustain their way of life.

From that day forward, the villagers worked tirelessly to expand and improve their underground network of tunnels and rooms. They knew that they could never be too prepared for the next eruption, but they also knew that they had the knowledge and resources to face any challenge that lay ahead.

And so, the warm volcanoes continued to provide for the villagers, fueling their passions and powering their lives, a symbol of the strength and resilience of the human spirit in the face of nature's power.

Read the story and fill in the blank spaces with the appropriate words.

The island of volcanoes

- In the heart of a lush tropical island lived a community of people who had learned to coexist with the warm _____ that surrounded their village.
- Every day, they would wake up to the gentle rumble of the earth beneath their feet and the _____ rising from the nearby mountains.
- The villagers had always known that life on this _____ was different from anywhere else.
- The warm volcanoes provided a natural source of energy that they used to _____ their food, heat their _____, and even power their _____.
- They had also learned how to harness the heat from the volcanoes to help grow their _____ and keep their animals warm during the cooler months.
- One day, as the villagers were tending to their fields, they noticed something strange happening around the _____ of one of the volcanoes.
- The ground was _____ violently, and steam was pouring out of the fissures in the earth.
- The villagers knew that this could only mean one thing, the volcano was about to _____.
- In a panic, the villagers ran towards the _____ to warn the others.
- They gathered in the _____ of the town, unsure of what to do next.

Read the story and circle whether the statement is true or false. If the statement is false, provide the correct answer for it.

The people who lived on the island had learned to coexist with the warm volcanoes.

True   False

The villagers woke up to the sound of thunder every morning.

True   False

The villagers used the heat from the volcanoes to cook their food, heat their homes, and even power their boats.

True   False

One day, the villagers noticed that one of the volcanoes was covered in snow.

True   False

An old man who had lived on the island for many years led the villagers to a large underground cave system.

True   False

The villagers were unprepared for the volcanic eruption.

True   False

Read the story 'The island of volcanoes' and answer the following questions.

How did the villagers coexist with the warm volcanoes on the island?

What natural source of energy did the villagers use to cook their food, heat their homes, and power their boats?

When the villagers noticed something strange happening around the base of one of the volcanoes, what was happening?

Who led the villagers to a large underground cave system that had been carved out around the base of one of the warm volcanoes?

What did the villagers do to prepare for the next eruption after the initial one had ceased?

> **Assess your reading fluency by writing the number of words read per minute.**

In the heart of a lush tropical island lived a community of people who had learned to coexist with the warm volcanoes that surrounded their village.	30
Every day, they would wake up to the gentle rumble of the earth beneath their feet and the steam rising from the nearby mountains.	50
The villagers had always known that life on this island was different from anywhere else.	65
The warm volcanoes provided a natural source of energy that they used to cook their food, heat their homes, and even power their boats.	89
They had also learned how to harness the heat from the volcanoes to help grow their crops and keep their animals warm during the cooler months.	115
One day, as the villagers were tending to their fields, they noticed something strange happening around the base of one of the volcanoes.	135
The ground was shaking violently, and steam was pouring out of the fissures in the earth.	154
The villagers knew that this could only mean one thing, the volcano was about to erupt.	170
In a panic, the villagers ran towards the village to warn the others.	183
They gathered in the center of the town, unsure of what to do next.	197
Suddenly, an old man stepped forward.	203
He had lived on the island for many years and had seen his fair share of volcanic eruptions.	221
"Everyone, calm down," he said. "We have been preparing for this moment for years. We know exactly what to do."	241
The villagers looked at the old man in disbelief. How could anyone be prepared for something like this?	259
The old man led the villagers to a large underground cave system that had been carved out around the base of one of the warm volcanoes.	385

Inside, they found a network of tunnels and rooms that had been built to withstand the heat and pressure of an eruption.	307
As the villagers huddled in the safety of the caves, they watched in awe as the volcano erupted outside.	326
Lava spewed from the top of the mountain, and ash rained down from the sky.	341
But the villagers were safe, protected by the secure walls of the underground caves.	355
When the eruption had ceased, the villagers emerged from the caves, unscathed and amazed at the power of the warm volcanoes.	376
They knew that they would continue to live in harmony with these natural wonders, using their warmth and energy to sustain their way of life.	401
From that day forward, the villagers worked tirelessly to expand and improve their underground network of tunnels and rooms.	420
They knew that they could never be too prepared for the next eruption, but they also knew that they had the knowledge and resources to face any challenge that lay ahead.	451
And so, the warm volcanoes continued to provide for the villagers, fueling their passions and powering their lives, a symbol of the strength and resilience of the human spirit in the face of nature's power.	486

Date			
Words per minute			
Number of errors			

Make sentences using the words written below.

Volcanoes
_____
_____

Erupt
_____
_____

Village
_____
_____

Mountain
_____
_____

Cave
_____
_____

Underground
_____
_____

> Make a story using only five verbs from the following.

lived   learned   coexist   wake up
rumble   rising   provide   cook   heat
power   grow   keep   noticed

Read the following sentences. Rewrite the sentences with correct punctuation.

1. the warm volcanoes on the Island provided a natural source of energy for the villagers

2. the warm Volcanoes continued to, be a symbol of the strength and resilience of the human spirit in the face of nature's power

3. the villagers learned to coexist with the volcanoes using their heat to grow crops and keep their animals warm

4. the ground shook violently as one of the volcanoes prepared to erupt

5. the villagers ran to find safety in a network of underground caves built to withstand the heat and pressure of an eruption

6. lava spewed from the top of the volcano, as ash rained down from the sky

7. the villagers emerged from the caves unscathed, grateful for the protection they had found

> Read the story and underline all the nouns and pronouns in the story written below. Use the underlined words to make a new sentence.

Volcanoes are fascinating natural phenomena that inspire both awe and fear. They can be found all around the world, from the towering peaks of the Rockies to the idyllic islands of the Pacific. At their core, volcanoes are massive geological structures that are formed by the accumulation of molten rock, ash, and other volcanic materials. Their sheer size and power make them objects of fascination for humans and other creatures alike. When a volcano erupts, it can unleash a torrent of fiery destruction, changing the landscape and affecting the lives of those living nearby. Nevertheless, they continue to be a source of wonder and inspiration for people everywhere.

Nouns	Pronouns	Sentences

Find and circle the words written below.

volcano   erupt   hot   warm
island   shaking   underground

h	e	r	u	p	t	w	e	d	w	n	u
e	c	l	i	o	b	a	c	a	e	u	n
a	n	a	h	i	m	r	l	s	l	t	d
l	e	y	t	g	p	m	g	e	b	r	e
i	s	l	a	n	d	c	j	a	a	i	r
h	t	e	r	t	e	e	g	l	t	c	g
y	i	g	s	s	t	s	y	t	e	i	r
a	u	t	e	i	a	s	r	h	g	o	o
s	h	a	k	i	n	g	a	y	e	n	u
f	q	o	o	d	m	p	m	j	v	c	n
k	x	v	o	l	c	a	n	o	n	p	d

> **Read the story. Identify and underline all the nouns in the story.**

Maggie's adventure

Maggie had always dreamed of living on a farm. She imagined herself surrounded by animals, fields of green, and a peaceful life. Her dream came true when she moved to the countryside and bought a small farm of her own.

At first, things were hard. Maggie was unaccustomed to the early mornings, the hard work, and the constant maintenance that came with running a farm. But she was determined to succeed, and so she persevered.

One day, while tending to her fields, Maggie stumbled upon a secret underground tunnel that led to a hidden cave system. She was amazed at what she found, stalagmites and stalactites, and even a small underground lake. She had no idea how long the cave had been there, or who had built it, but she knew that she had to explore it further.

Over the next few weeks, Maggie ventured deeper into the cave, exploring its twists and turns and discovering new wonders at every turn. She even found a rare species of mushrooms growing in the damp earth that she was able to sell at the market for a good profit.

One day, as Maggie was exploring the cave, she heard a strange noise coming from a nearby tunnel. She followed the sound, cautiously moving deeper into the darkness. As she rounded a corner, she was suddenly face-to-face with a large, ferocious-looking beast!

Maggie froze, unsure of what to do. But then she remembered something her grandfather had told her, when faced with danger, never show fear. So she stood tall and faced the beast head-on.

To her surprise, the beast didn't attack. Instead, it let out a low growl and slowly backed away, disappearing into the darkness.

> **Read the story. Identify and underline all the nouns in the story.**

Maggie was ecstatic. She had faced her fears and come out unscathed. From that day forward, she continued to explore the cave system, discovering new wonders, and making new friends with the creatures that called it home.

As time went on, Maggie's farm became well-known for its unique mushrooms and the strange underground cave system that lay beneath it. Visitors came from far and wide to explore the cave and taste the delicious produce grown on the farm.

Maggie had come a long way from her city life, but she knew that she had found the perfect place to call home. She had discovered the joys of farm life, hard work, adventure, and unexpected surprises around every corner, and she wouldn't have it any other way.

Read the story and fill in the blank spaces with the appropriate words.

Maggie's adventure

- _____ had always dreamed of living on a farm.
- She imagined herself surrounded by _____, fields of green, and a peaceful life.
- Her dream came true when she moved to the _____ and bought a small farm of her own.
- Maggie was unaccustomed to the early mornings, the hard _____, and the constant maintenance that came with running a farm.
- But she was determined to _____, and so she persevered.
- One day, while tending to her fields, Maggie stumbled upon a secret underground _____ that led to a hidden cave system.
- She was amazed at what she found, stalagmites and stalactites, and even a small underground _____.
- She had no idea how long the _____ had been there, or who had built it, but she knew that she had to explore it further.
- Over the next few weeks, Maggie ventured deeper into the cave, exploring its _____ and turns and discovering new wonders at every turn.
- She even found a rare species of _____ growing in the damp earth that she was able to sell at the market for a good profit.
- One day, as Maggie was exploring the cave, she heard a strange noise coming from a nearby tunnel. She followed the sound, cautiously moving deeper into the darkness. As she rounded a corner, she was suddenly face-to-face with a large, ferocious-looking _____!

Read the story and circle whether the statement is true or false. If the statement is false, provide the correct answer for it.

Maggie regretted her decision to leave the city and move to the countryside.

True   False

Running a farm was easy for Maggie and required little effort.

True   False

Maggie discovered a secret underground tunnel that led to a hidden cave system while tending to her fields.

True   False

The cave system was devoid of any interesting features or creatures.

True   False

When Maggie encountered the ferocious-looking beast in the cave, it attacked her.

True   False

Visitors came from far and wide to explore the cave system and taste the produce grown on Maggie's farm.

True   False

Read the story 'Maggie's adventures' and answer the following questions.

What motivated Maggie to leave the city and move to the countryside to start a farm?

_____
_____
_____

How did Maggie discover the hidden cave system on her farm, and what did she find inside?

_____
_____
_____
_____

What advice did Maggie's grandfather give her that helped her when faced with danger in the cave?

_____
_____
_____
_____
_____

How did Maggie's farm become well-known, and what drew visitors to it?

_____
_____
_____
_____
_____
_____

What did Maggie discover about herself and the joys of farm life through her adventures on the farm and in the cave system?

_____
_____
_____
_____

Assess your reading fluency by writing the number of words read per minute.

Maggie had always dreamed of living on a farm.	9
She imagined herself surrounded by animals, fields of green, and a peaceful life.	22
Her dream came true when she moved to the countryside and bought a small farm of her own.	40
At first, things were hard. Maggie was unaccustomed to the early mornings, the hard work, and the constant maintenance that came with running a farm.	65
But she was determined to succeed, and so she persevered.	75
She was amazed at what she found, stalagmites and stalactites, and even a small underground lake.	113
She had no idea how long the cave had been there, or who had built it, but she knew that she had to explore it further.	138
Over the next few weeks, Maggie ventured deeper into the cave, exploring its twists and turns and discovering new wonders at every turn.	161
She even found a rare species of mushrooms growing in the damp earth that she was able to sell at the market for a good profit.	187
One day, as Maggie was exploring the cave, she heard a strange noise coming from a nearby tunnel.	205
She followed the sound, cautiously moving deeper into the darkness.	215
As she rounded a corner, she was suddenly face-to-face with a large, ferocious-looking beast!	221
Maggie froze, unsure of what to do. But then she remembered something her grandfather had told her, when faced with danger, never show fear.	253
So she stood tall and faced the beast head-on.	269

To her surprise, the beast didn't attack.	
Instead, it let out a low growl and slowly backed away, disappearing into the darkness.	284
Maggie was ecstatic.	287
She had faced her fears and come out unscathed.	296
From that day forward, she continued to explore the cave system, discovering new wonders, and making new friends with the creatures that called it home.	321
As time went on, Maggie's farm became well-known for its unique mushrooms and the strange underground cave system that lay beneath it.	344
Visitors came from far and wide to explore the cave and taste the delicious produce grown on the farm.	362
Maggie had come a long way from her city life, but she knew that she had found the perfect place to call home.	385
She had discovered the joys of farm life, hard work, adventure, and unexpected surprises around every corner, and she wouldn't have it any other way.	410

Date			
Words per minute			
Number of errors			

Make sentences using the words written below.

Farm

Animals

Beast

Cave

Underground

Twists

> Make a story using only five verbs from the following.

dreamed   imagined   moved   bought   were   was   tending   stumbled   led   found   was   explored

> Underline the adjectives in the following sentences. Use the underlined adjective to make a new sentence.

1. The cows lazily grazed in the pastures, enjoying the warm sun on their hides.

2. The chickens clucked contentedly as they scratched around in the dirt, searching for tasty bugs and worms.

1. The horses stood at attention, their ears perked up as they listened for any signs of danger.

2. The pigs snorted happily as they rolled around in the mud, their pink skin glistening in the sunlight.

3. The goats climbed up onto piles of hay, nibbling on the sweet grasses and leaves that poked out from the bales.

4. The sheep huddled together for warmth, their woolly coats keeping them cozy on cold winter nights.

5. The ducks quacked as they splashed around in the pond, diving down to catch fish in their beaks.

Read the story and write the synonyms and antonyms of the underlined words. Use the underlined words to make new sentences.

Farm animals are an <u>essential</u> part of the agricultural industry, <u>providing</u> food, wool, eggs, and many other products that people depend on every day. From cows and pigs to chickens and goats, each animal has its <u>unique</u> characteristics and benefits. Cows are <u>raised</u> for their milk and meat, while pigs provide pork, bacon, and ham. Chickens <u>produce</u> eggs, and their meat is also <u>popular</u> in many cuisines. Goats are known for their milk, cheese, and meat, as well as their ability to <u>clear</u> land of unwanted vegetation. Horses are used for transportation and work on farms, while sheep produce wool and meat. Each animal requires <u>care</u> and attention, from proper nutrition and <u>shelter</u> to regular medical checkups. Many farmers develop close relationships with their animals, often <u>giving</u> them names and taking pride in their health and well-being. Farm animals play an important role in our world, and without them, our lives would be very different.

S.No	Synonyms	Antonyms	Sentences
1			
2			
3			
4			
5			
6			
7			
8			
9			
10			

Find and circle the words written below.

farm   animals   love
countryside   horses   pig
sheep

f	i	v	e	r	c	h	o	m	e	a	g
r	a	n	i	m	a	l	s	j	o	i	r
e	s	r	s	i	m	o	e	i	p	e	e
k	l	v	m	g	p	v	g	h	k	n	a
r	e	e	a	k	b	e	c	l	e	e	n
o	n	r	r	y	b	r	g	e	r	c	a
n	n	r	p	n	a	s	q	e	s	p	e
o	a	n	e	e	i	s	i	o	n	l	c
z	h	y	e	a	m	i	d	s	a	m	o
a	c	m	h	t	l	a	n	t	i	c	y
h	o	r	s	s	u	i	l	t	c	b	v
c	o	u	n	t	r	y	s	i	d	e	o

Read the story. Identify and underline all the verbs in the story.

Creepy crawlers

Lila had always been fascinated by insects and creepy crawlers. She loved observing their behavior and learning about their unique characteristics. Her love for these creatures started when she was a child, and she would spend hours exploring the garden, looking under rocks and logs for any sign of bugs.

As she grew older, Lila's fascination with insects only intensified. She spent her weekends volunteering at the local insect exhibit, where she helped care for the many different species on display. She learned about the incredible diversity of insects, from the delicate butterfly to the ferocious praying mantis.

One day, while hiking in the woods, Lila stumbled upon a large nest of ants. She watched in amazement as hundreds of tiny ants swarmed around her feet, carrying bits of leaves and other materials back to the nest. She knew that ants worked in an organized and efficient manner, but seeing it firsthand was truly awe-inspiring.

As Lila continued her hike, she came across a giant spider web spanning the length of a tree. The spider was nowhere to be seen, but its intricate web was a work of art. Lila took a few pictures and continued her journey, her mind buzzing with excitement at all the new discoveries she was making.

Over the next few months, Lila continued to explore the world of insects and creepy crawlers. She encountered beetles, centipedes, and even a venomous scorpion. Each new discovery was like a puzzle piece, fitting into the larger picture of the complex ecosystem that existed all around her.

> **Read the story. Identify and underline all the verbs in the story.**

One day, Lila <u>was approached</u> by a group of scientists who <u>were studying</u> the behavior of fireflies. They <u>asked</u> if she <u>would be</u> interested in helping them <u>collect</u> data on the insects, and Lila eagerly <u>agreed</u>.

For weeks, Lila <u>spent</u> her evenings in the fields, gently <u>catching</u> fireflies and <u>recording</u> their behavior. She <u>learned</u> about their mating habits, their attraction to light, and their unique bioluminescence. It <u>was</u> a magical experience, being <u>surrounded</u> by so many glowing insects, and Lila <u>felt</u> like she <u>was</u> part of something truly special.

As the summer <u>came</u> to an end, Lila <u>knew</u> that her time with the insects <u>was ending</u>. But she also <u>knew</u> that her love for these creatures would never <u>fade</u>. For Lila, every insect and creepy crawler <u>was</u> a marvel of nature, a unique and fascinating piece of the ecosystem that <u>made</u> our world so incredibly diverse and wondrous.

> **Read the story and fill in the blank spaces with the appropriate words.**

Creepy crawlers

- Lila had always been fascinated by _____ and creepy crawlers. She loved observing their behavior and learning about their unique _____.
- Her love for these creatures started when she was a child, and she would spend hours exploring the _____, looking under rocks and logs for any sign of _____.
- As she grew older, Lila's fascination with insects only _____.
- She spent her weekends volunteering at the local _____, where she helped care for the many different species on display.
- She learned about the incredible diversity of insects, from the delicate _____ to the ferocious praying _____.
- One day, while hiking in the woods, Lila stumbled upon a large _____ of ants.
- She watched in amazement as hundreds of tiny ants swarmed around her feet, carrying bits of _____ and other materials back to the nest.
- She knew that ants worked in an _____ and efficient manner but seeing it firsthand was truly awe-inspiring.
- As Lila continued her hike, she came across a giant _____ web spanning the length of a tree.
- The spider was nowhere to be seen, but its intricate _____ was a work of art.
- Lila took a few _____ and continued her journey, her mind buzzing with excitement at all the new discoveries she was making.

Read the story and circle whether the statement is true or false. If the statement is false, provide the correct answer for it.

Lila lost interest in studying insects as the summer came to an end.

True   False

Lila volunteered at a local insect exhibit to learn more about different species of insects.

True   False

While hiking in the woods, Lila encountered a large nest of bees.

True   False

Lila was amazed by the organized and efficient manner in which the ants worked together.

True   False

Lila discovered a giant spider web while hiking in the woods, but she did not see the spider.

True   False

Lila agreed to help a group of scientists collect data on the behavior of fireflies.

True   False

Read the story 'Creepy crawlers' and answer the following questions.

How did Lila's love for insects and creepy crawlers begin, and what inspired her fascination with these creatures?

_____
_____
_____
_____

What did Lila learn while volunteering at the local insect exhibit, and how did this experience contribute to her knowledge of different species of insects??

_____
_____
_____
_____
_____

Describe the encounter Lila had with a large group of ants while hiking in the woods, and what amazed her most about their behavior.

_____
_____
_____
_____
_____

How did Lila's involvement in the firefly research project contribute to her understanding of these insects, and what did she discover about their unique characteristics?

_____
_____
_____
_____
_____

How did Lila's appreciation for insects and creepy crawlers evolve over time, and what did she learn about the important role they play in our ecosystem?

_____
_____
_____
_____
_____

Assess your reading fluency by writing the number of words read per minute.

Lila had always been fascinated by insects and creepy crawlers.	10
She loved observing their behavior and learning about their unique characteristics.	21
Her love for these creatures started when she was a child, and she would spend hours exploring the garden, looking under rocks and logs for any sign of bugs.	50
As she grew older, Lila's fascination with insects only intensified.	61
She spent her weekends volunteering at the local insect exhibit, where she helped care for the many different species on display.	81
She learned about the incredible diversity of insects, from the delicate butterfly to the ferocious praying mantis.	98
One day, while hiking in the woods, Lila stumbled upon a large nest of ants.	113
She watched in amazement as hundreds of tiny ants swarmed around her feet, carrying bits of leaves and other materials back to the nest.	138
She knew that ants worked in an organized and efficient manner, but seeing it firsthand was truly awe-inspiring.	155
As Lila continued her hike, she came across a giant spider web spanning the length of a tree.	174
The spider was nowhere to be seen, but its intricate web was a work of art.	189
Lila took a few pictures and continued her journey, her mind buzzing with excitement at all the new discoveries she was making.	221
Over the next few months, Lila continued to explore the world of insects and creepy crawlers. She encountered beetles, centipedes, and even a venomous scorpion.	236

One day, Lila was approached by a group of scientists who were studying the behavior of fireflies.	275
At first, Rachel was terrified, after all, these were some of the most fearsome predators on the planet.	293
But as she watched from a safe distance, she couldn't help but be struck by the beauty and majesty of these magnificent creatures.	316
As the journey came to an end and Rachel made her way back to civilization, she knew that she had experienced something truly special.	341
As the summer came to an end, Lila knew that her time with the insects was ending.	364
But she also knew that her love for these creatures would never fade.	377
For Lila, every insect and creepy crawler was a marvel of nature, a unique and fascinating piece of the ecosystem that made our world so incredibly diverse and wondrous characteristics.	407

Date			
Words per minute			
Number of errors			

Make sentences using the words written below.

Insects

Creepy

Crawlers

Spiders

Ants

Nest

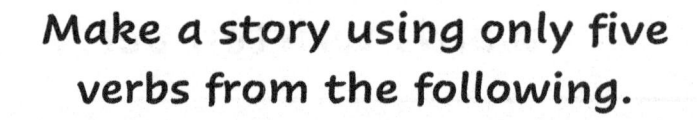

> Make a story using only five verbs from the following.

**loved   observing   learning   grew
spent   exploring   looking   stumbled
watched   knew   worked**

> Underline the adjectives in the following sentences. Use the underlined adjective to make a new sentence.

1. The <u>iridescent</u> wings of the butterfly shimmered in the sunlight as it fluttered among the flowers.

1. The <u>industrious</u> ants worked tirelessly to build their intricate nest from tiny bits of leaves and dirt.

2. The <u>delicate</u> dragonfly hovered gracefully in the air, its long, slender body glistening in the sun.

3. The <u>furry</u> caterpillar inched its way along the tree trunk, leaving a trail of soft, green fuzz behind.

4. The <u>prickly</u> legs of the spider clung tightly to its web as it waited patiently for its next meal.

5. The <u>slimy</u> tentacles of the snail left glistening trails on the leaves as it made its way across the garden.

6. The <u>vibrant</u> colors of the beetle's shell sparkled in the light, catching the eye of anyone who walked by.

7. The <u>buzzing</u> wings of the bee hummed steadily as it flitted from flower to flower, collecting pollen.

8. The <u>sharp</u> pincers of the scorpion glinted menacingly in the moonlight, ready to defend itself against any predator.

9. The <u>creepy</u> crawly centipede scurried along the ground, its many legs propelling it forward in quick bursts of movement.

> Read the story and write the synonyms and antonyms of the underlined words. Use the underlined words to make new sentences.

Lila had always been fascinated by insects and creepy crawlers. She <u>loved</u> <u>observing</u> their behavior and learning about their <u>unique</u> characteristics. Her love for these creatures started when she was a <u>child</u>, and she would <u>spend</u> hours exploring the garden, looking <u>under</u> rocks and logs for any sign of bugs.

As she grew <u>older</u>, Lila's fascination with insects only <u>intensified</u>. She spent her weekends volunteering at the <u>local</u> insect exhibit, where she helped <u>care</u> for the many different species on display. She learned about the incredible diversity of insects, from the delicate butterfly to the ferocious praying mantis.

S.No	Synonyms	Antonyms	Sentences
1			
2			
3			
4			
5			
6			
7			
8			
9			
10			

Find and circle the words written below.

creepy   crawlers   insects
ants   spiders   species   firefly

p	f	i	r	e	f	l	y	r	s	p	i
s	b	f	r	o	z	e	n	j	r	l	n
e	s	s	i	g	n	e	d	l	e	a	s
i	r	c	t	g	u	e	g	h	d	n	e
c	e	i	l	d	l	i	f	e	i	e	c
e	l	e	r	y	o	r	g	e	p	l	t
p	w	r	e	n	p	s	q	a	s	l	s
s	a	j	a	c	x	s	i	o	n	o	n
c	r	r	e	e	z	i	n	g	s	t	a
o	c	r	e	e	p	y	t	n	r	e	s

Read the story. Identify and underline all the verbs in the story.

Heritage of Native American culture

The history of Native Americans is a rich and complex tapestry of cultures, languages, traditions, and spiritual beliefs that stretches back thousands of years. Before the arrival of European explorers and settlers, there were hundreds of different tribes and nations across what is now known as North America. These groups were diverse in their customs, but they all shared a deep connection to the land, the natural world, and their ancestral heritage.

Native American societies were organized around kinship and clan relationships, with extended families living in communal villages or nomadic bands. Tribes often had their own distinct languages, customs, and spiritual practices, ranging from animistic beliefs in the power of nature spirits to elaborate cosmologies involving multiple deities.

These groups flourished for centuries, developing sophisticated systems of agriculture, trade, and governance that enabled them to thrive in a wide variety of environments. From the lush forests of the Pacific Northwest to the arid deserts of the Southwest, Native American communities adapted to their surroundings, utilizing the resources of the land to meet their needs and sustain their way of life.

However, the arrival of European explorers and colonizers in the 16th and 17th centuries had devastating consequences for Native American societies. Diseases brought by Europeans decimated populations, while wars, forced relocation, and cultural assimilation efforts aimed at erasing native culture and language left lasting scars.

> **Read the story. Identify and underline all the verbs in the story.**

Despite these challenges, Native American communities continue to preserve their cultural heritage and traditions in the face of ongoing struggles for land rights, sovereignty, and recognition of their unique place in American history. The Native American Rights Fund, founded in 1970, has been instrumental in advocating for the legal rights of Native American communities, including protections for sacred sites, access to education and healthcare, and recognition of tribal sovereignty.

Today, Native American cultures and traditions are celebrated and honored through powwows, art exhibitions, museum exhibits, and other forms of cultural expression. Many tribes have also become leaders in environmental and conservation efforts, recognizing the critical importance of preserving natural resources and traditional lands for future generations.

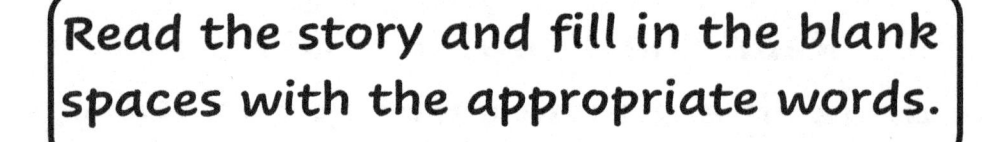

Read the story and fill in the blank spaces with the appropriate words.

Heritage of Native American culture

- The history of Native Americans is a rich and complex tapestry of cultures, languages, _____, and spiritual beliefs that stretches back thousands of years.
- Before the arrival of _____ explorers and settlers, there were hundreds of different tribes and nations across what is now known as North America.
- These groups were diverse in their customs, but they all shared a deep connection to the land, the natural world, and their _____.
- Native American societies were organized around _____ and clan relationships, with extended families living in communal villages or nomadic bands.
- Tribes often had their own distinct languages, customs, and spiritual practices, ranging from _____ beliefs in the power of nature spirits to elaborate cosmologies involving multiple deities.
- These groups flourished for centuries, developing sophisticated systems of _____, _____, and governance that enabled them to thrive in a wide variety of environments.
- From the lush forests of the _____ to the arid deserts of the Southwest, Native American communities adapted to their surroundings, utilizing the resources of the land to meet their needs and sustain their way of life.
- However, the arrival of European explorers and colonizers in the _____ and _____ centuries had devastating consequences for Native American societies.

Read the story and circle whether the statement is true or false. If the statement is false, provide the correct answer for it.

Native American societies were highly diverse and varied in their customs and spiritual beliefs.

True   False

_____

Before the arrival of Europeans, there were no organized tribes or nations across North America.

True   False

_____

Native American communities adapted to their surroundings by using the resources of the land to sustain their way of life.

True   False

_____

The arrival of European explorers and settlers had no significant impact on Native American populations or cultures.

True   False

_____

Many Native American tribes have become leaders in environmental and conservation efforts.

True   False

_____

Read the story 'Heritage of Native American culture' and answer the following questions.

How were Native American societies organized before European arrival?
_____
_____
_____
_____

What were some of the spiritual beliefs and customs that were shared among various Native American tribes and nations?
_____
_____
_____
_____
_____

What were some of the challenges that Native American communities faced after European contact?
_____
_____
_____
_____
_____
_____

What is the Native American Rights Fund and what kind of work do they do?
_____
_____
_____
_____
_____
_____
_____

How have Native American communities continued to preserve their cultural heritage and traditions in the face of ongoing struggles for land rights, sovereignty, and recognition?
_____
_____
_____
_____

Assess your reading fluency by writing the number of words read per minute.

The history of Native Americans is a rich and complex tapestry of cultures, languages, traditions, and spiritual beliefs that stretches back thousands of years.	24
Before the arrival of European explorers and settlers, there were hundreds of different tribes and nations across what is now known as North America.	48
These groups were diverse in their customs, but they all shared a deep connection to the land, the natural world, and their ancestral heritage.	72
Native American societies were organized around kinship and clan relationships, with extended families living in communal villages or nomadic bands.	92
Tribes often had their own distinct languages, customs, and spiritual practices, ranging from animistic beliefs in the power of nature spirits to elaborate cosmologies involving multiple deities.	119
These groups flourished for centuries, developing sophisticated systems of agriculture, trade, and governance that enabled them to thrive in a wide variety of environments.	143
From the lush forests of the Pacific Northwest to the arid deserts of the Southwest, Native American communities adapted to their surroundings, utilizing the resources of the land to meet their needs and sustain their way of life.	181
However, the arrival of European explorers and colonizers in the 16th and 17th centuries had devastating consequences for Native American societies.	203
Diseases brought by Europeans decimated populations, while wars, forced relocation, and cultural assimilation efforts aimed at erasing native culture and language left lasting scars.	226

Despite these challenges, Native American communities continue to preserve their cultural heritage and traditions in the face of ongoing struggles for land rights, sovereignty, and recognition of their unique place in American history.	259
The Native American Rights Fund, founded in 1970, has been instrumental in advocating for the legal rights of Native American communities, including protections for sacred sites, access to education and healthcare, and recognition of tribal sovereignty.	295
Today, Native American cultures and traditions are celebrated and honored through powwows, art exhibitions, museum exhibits, and other forms of cultural expression.	317
Many tribes have also become leaders in environmental and conservation efforts, recognizing the critical importance of preserving natural resources and traditional lands for future generations.	342

Date			
Words per minute			
Number of errors			

Make sentences using the words written below.

American

Native

History

Heritage

Villages

Population

Make a story using only five verbs from the following.

stretches   shared   connected
organized   living   adapting
utilizing   flourished   developing

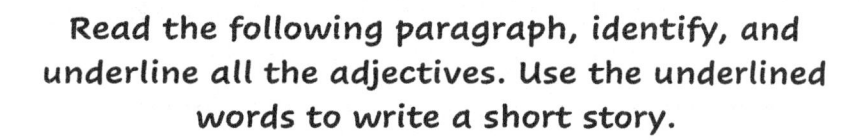

> **Read the following paragraph, identify, and underline all the adjectives. Use the underlined words to write a short story.**

Native American cultures are diverse, intricate, and deeply connected to the land. They are characterized by rich spiritual traditions, complex kinship systems, and a deep reverence for nature. Native American communities are known for their resilience, adaptability, and resourcefulness in the face of adversity. They have developed sophisticated systems of agriculture, trade, and governance that allowed them to thrive in a wide range of environments. These communities are also known for their artistic expressions, including pottery, weaving, beadwork, and storytelling, which are passed down from generation to generation. The enduring legacy of Native American cultures is one that is marked by tradition, creativity, and a powerful connection to the natural world.

Story

Read the following paragraph, identify, and underline all the conjunctions. Use the conjunctions to make sentences.

Native American history is a complex and multifaceted tapestry that spans thousands of years. It is a story of diverse people and cultures, connected by a shared heritage and a deep reverence for the natural world. Native American societies were organized in a variety of ways, with distinct kinship systems, political structures, and spiritual beliefs. They lived off the land, adapting to their surroundings and utilizing its resources in innovative ways. Over time, Native American communities faced a range of challenges, including decimation, displacement, and forced assimilation. However, they continue to preserve their cultural heritage and traditions, advocating for their legal rights and addressing ongoing social and environmental issues. The story of Native American history is one that is marked by resilience, creativity, and an enduring commitment to community and the natural world.

Conjunctions	Sentences

Find and circle the words written below.

American native history
tradition culture heritage

c	h	e	r	i	t	a	g	e	c	a	h
d	c	w	a	l	k	s	q	j	e	p	i
e	o	c	s	i	s	b	p	i	s	a	s
r	r	h	t	g	o	e	g	v	e	m	t
u	a	m	e	r	i	c	a	n	i	r	o
t	l	r	r	a	i	r	k	a	c	h	r
l	f	i	s	h	e	c	r	t	f	t	y
u	t	u	r	t	l	e	s	i	n	a	v
c	m	f	i	r	s	t	r	v	s	e	i
u	n	t	r	a	d	i	t	i	o	n	d

Read the story. Identify and underline all the verbs in the story.

A trip to the zoo

As I walked through the gates of the zoo, I felt a wave of excitement wash over me. It had been years since I had visited a zoo and I was eager to see all the animals up close and personal. The sun was shining, and families were milling about, laughing and chatting as they enjoyed their day out. The first exhibit I came across was the lion enclosure. I could hear the deep rumble of their growls as I approached, and my heart began to race with anticipation.

The lions were magnificent creatures, with their golden manes and piercing eyes. They lay lazily in the sun, occasionally stretching a paw or flicking their tails. As I watched, one of the males suddenly rose to his feet and let out an earth-shattering roar. I jumped back in surprise but couldn't help but feel a sense of awe at the sheer power of the beast.

Moving on, I came across the monkey exhibit. The monkeys were playful and mischievous, swinging from vines and chasing each other around. One little monkey even stopped to give me a curious look before scampering off to join its friends. I couldn't help but smile at their antics, and I spent a good half-hour watching them play.

Next up was the reptile house, which I approached with a mixture of curiosity and trepidation. I've always found snakes and lizards a little unsettling, but I wanted to challenge myself. As I peered into the glass enclosures, I was surprised to find that I was fascinated by the variety of shapes and colors of the different species. From the bright green iguanas to the sleek black cobras, each creature had its own unique beauty.

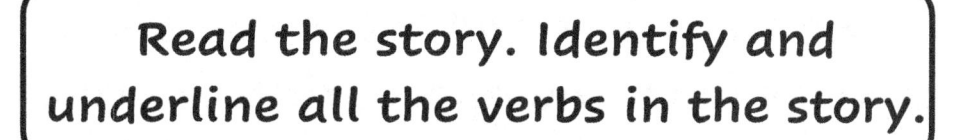

> **Read the story. Identify and underline all the verbs in the story.**

As the afternoon <u>wore</u> on, I <u>made</u> my way to the giraffe exhibit. I <u>had</u> always <u>loved</u> these gentle giants, with their long necks and soulful eyes. <u>Seeing</u> them in real life <u>was</u> even more awe-inspiring than I <u>had imagined</u>. They <u>were grazing</u> on tall branches, their tongues <u>flicking</u> out to <u>pluck</u> the leaves as they <u>towered</u> above me. I <u>felt</u> a sense of peacefulness <u>wash</u> over me as I <u>watched</u> them, and for a moment, I <u>forgot</u> about all my worries.

As the day <u>drew</u> to a close, I <u>made</u> my way back to the entrance, <u>feeling</u> tired but fulfilled. The zoo <u>had been</u> an amazing experience, and I <u>felt</u> grateful to <u>have had</u> the chance to <u>witness</u> so many incredible creatures in one place. As I <u>walked</u> out, I <u>couldn't help</u> but <u>think</u> about the importance of conservation and <u>protecting</u> these animals and their habitats for future generations to <u>enjoy</u>.

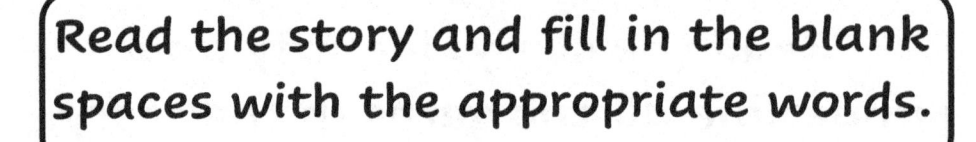

A trip to the zoo

- As I walked through the gates of the _____, I felt a wave of excitement wash over me. It had been years since I had visited a zoo and I was eager to see all the animals up close and personal.
- The sun was shining, and families were milling about, _____ and chatting as they enjoyed their day out.
- The first exhibit I came across was the _____ enclosure. I could hear the deep rumble of their growls as I approached, and my heart began to race with anticipation.
- The lions were magnificent creatures, with their golden manes and piercing _____. They lay lazily in the sun, occasionally stretching a paw or _____ their tails.
- As I watched, one of the males suddenly rose to his feet and let out an earth-shattering _____.
- I jumped back in surprise but couldn't help but feel a sense of awe at the sheer power of the _____.
- Moving on, I came across the _____ exhibit. The monkeys were playful and _____, swinging from vines and chasing each other around.
- One little monkey even stopped to give me a _____ look before scampering off to join its friends.
- I couldn't help but smile at their _____, and I spent a good half-hour watching them play.
- Next up was the _____ house, which I approached with a mixture of curiosity and trepidation.
- I've always found _____ and _____ a little unsettling, but I wanted to challenge myself.

Read the story and circle whether the statement is true or false. If the statement is false, provide the correct answer for it.

The narrator was excited to visit the zoo but felt apprehensive about some of the exhibits.

True   False

The lions in the zoo were friendly and enjoyed interacting with visitors.

True   False

The monkey exhibit was full of playful and energetic primates.

True   False

The reptile house was the narrator's favorite exhibit at the zoo.

True   False

Seeing the giraffes up close left the narrator feeling peaceful and fulfilled.

True   False

The Johnson family made a new tradition to visit the zoo every year.

True   False

Read the story 'A trip to the zoo' and answer the following questions.

What was the narrator's initial reaction upon entering the zoo?

Which exhibit did the narrator find the most unsettling?

What was the narrator's favorite animal at the zoo and why?

How did the narrator feel after spending the day at the zoo?

What lesson did the narrator learn from visiting the zoo?

Assess your reading fluency by writing the number of words read per minute.

As I walked through the gates of the zoo, I felt a wave of excitement wash over me.	18
It had been years since I had visited a zoo and I was eager to see all the animals up close and personal.	41
The sun was shining, and families were milling about, laughing and chatting as they enjoyed their day out.	59
The first exhibit I came across was the lion enclosure.	69
I could hear the deep rumble of their growls as I approached, and my heart began to race with anticipation.	89
The lions were magnificent creatures, with their golden manes and piercing eyes.	101
They lay lazily in the sun, occasionally stretching a paw or flicking their tails.	115
As I watched, one of the males suddenly rose to his feet and let out an earth-shattering roar.	133
I jumped back in surprise but couldn't help but feel a sense of awe at the sheer power of the beast.	154
Moving on, I came across the monkey exhibit.	162
After the lions, the family made their way to the elephant exhibit.	204
The monkeys were playful and mischievous, swinging from vines and chasing each other around.	176
One little monkey even stopped to give me a curious look before scampering off to join its friends.	194
I couldn't help but smile at their antics, and I spent a good half-hour watching them play.	211
Next up was the reptile house, which I approached with a mixture of curiosity and trepidation.	227

I've always found snakes and lizards a little unsettling, but I wanted to challenge myself.	242
As I peered into the glass enclosures, I was surprised to find that I was fascinated by the variety of shapes and colors of the different species.	269
From the bright green iguanas to the sleek black cobras, each creature had its own unique beauty.	286
As the afternoon wore on, I made my way to the giraffe exhibit.	299
I had always loved these gentle giants, with their long necks and soulful eyes.	313
Seeing them in real life was even more awe-inspiring than I had imagined.	326
They were grazing on tall branches, their tongues flicking out to pluck the leaves as they towered above me.	345
I felt a sense of peacefulness wash over me as I watched them, and for a moment, I forgot about all my worries.	368
As the day drew to a close, I made my way back to the entrance, feeling tired but fulfilled.	387
The zoo had been an amazing experience, and I felt grateful to have had the chance to witness so many incredible creatures in one place.	412
As I walked out, I couldn't help but think about the importance of conservation and protecting these animals and their habitats for future generations to enjoy.	438

Date			
Words per minute			
Number of errors			

Make sentences using the words written below.

Zoo

Animals

Exhibit

Girafe

Monkey

Reptile

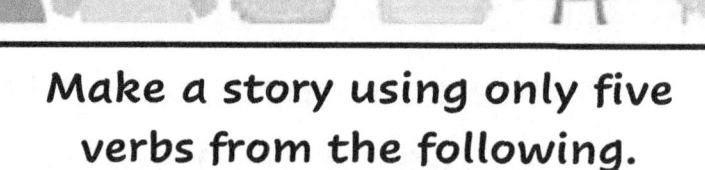

> Make a story using only five verbs from the following.

walked   felt   visited   approached
shining   milling   enjoyed   came   could
hear   growls   watched

Read the following paragraph and underline all the adjectives. Use any five adjectives from the paragraph to write a story in your own words.

The lions were the undisputed kings of the savannah, their golden coats shining brilliantly in the sunlight. Their fierce eyes glinted with intelligence as they surveyed the world around them. They were powerful, agile creatures, capable of chasing down prey with deadly skill. Their roars reverberated through the landscape, a symbol of their dominance and strength. However, there was more to the lions than just their ferocity. They were loyal and protective of their pride, caring for their cubs with tenderness and devotion. Watching them interact with one another, it was clear that these majestic creatures were more than just fearsome predators; they were intelligent, social beings with a deep capacity for empathy and love.

Story

Read the following story and underline all the nouns and pronouns. Use any five of the underlined words from the paragraph to write a story in your own words.

Monkeys are fascinating creatures, with their playful antics and curious nature. They are incredibly intelligent, using tools to solve problems and communicate with one another. Watching them swing from branch to branch, it's easy to see why they capture our imaginations. Their expressive eyes and nimble fingers make them seem almost human at times. However, we must remember that monkeys are still wild animals, and should be treated with respect and caution. Even though they may appear friendly, it's important to keep a safe distance and appreciate them from afar. Monkeys belong in their natural habitat, and it's up to us to preserve their homes and ensure they continue to thrive for generations to come.

Story

Find and circle the words written below.

zoo giraffe exhibit enjoy
reptiles roar beast
elephant

e	z	o	o	x	h	p	x	i	t	y	g
l	m	e	n	j	o	y	a	n	i	m	i
e	s	h	l	i	m	p	i	n	b	e	r
p	e	p	i	y	p	e	n	v	i	m	a
h	l	a	r	n	t	c	g	l	h	n	f
a	i	r	p	a	n	e	s	e	x	c	f
n	t	l	e	e	p	i	q	e	e	z	e
t	p	e	j	l	u	j	n	c	v	b	o
z	e	l	o	r	f	u	l	g	t	w	i
a	r	o	a	r	l	b	e	a	s	t	l

> **Read the story. Identify and underline all the verbs in the story.**

Sports camp

The school had organized a sports camp for the third graders during the summer holidays. The idea was to keep the children physically active, while also giving them an opportunity to learn new skills and make new friends.

As I approached the field where the camp was being held, I could see dozens of children running around, laughing, and shouting with enthusiasm. The coaches were doing an excellent job of keeping the children engaged, with a variety of fun games and activities.

There was a soccer station where the children were practicing their dribbling and shooting skills. Another station had them throwing and catching balls with precision and accuracy. Yet another station had them racing each other in relay races, their faces flushed with excitement.

I was impressed by the camaraderie amongst the children, as they cheered each other on and congratulated one another on their successes. It was clear that they were enjoying themselves, and I couldn't help but smile at the sight.

As the day wore on, the coaches introduced more complex drills and exercises, pushing the children to test their limits and work together as a team. Even those who were initially hesitant or shy had loosened up and were fully participating, thanks to the supportive environment created by the coaches.

I was particularly impressed by one little girl who had been struggling with the soccer drills earlier in the day. With encouragement from her teammates and the coaches, she persisted and eventually scored a goal, much to the delight of everyone watching.

Read the story. Identify and underline all the verbs in the story.

As the camp ended, the children gathered around the coaches for a group photo. They were sweaty and tired, but their faces were lit up with pride and accomplishment. The coaches handed out certificates and medals, recognizing each child's unique contributions and achievements. As I walked away from the camp, I couldn't help but feel grateful for the experience. The sports camp had not only kept the children active and healthy but had also taught them valuable life skills such as teamwork, perseverance, and sportsmanship. It was a wonderful example of how sports can be used as a tool for personal growth and development.

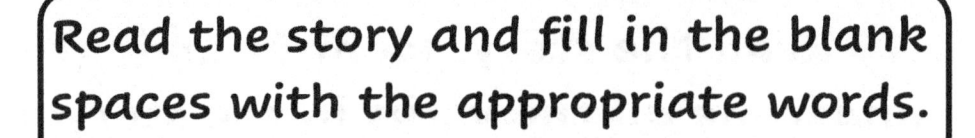

Read the story and fill in the blank spaces with the appropriate words.

Sports camp

- The school had organized a _____ camp for the third graders during the summer holidays.
- The idea was to keep the children _____ active, while also giving them an opportunity to learn new skills and make new friends.
- As I approached the _____ where the camp was being held, I could see dozens of children running around, laughing, and shouting with enthusiasm.
- The _____ were doing an excellent job of keeping the children engaged, with a variety of fun games and activities.
- There was a _____ where the children were practicing their dribbling and shooting skills.
- Another station had them _____ and catching balls with precision and accuracy.
- Yet another station had them racing each other in _____ _____, their faces flushed with excitement.
- I was impressed by the _____ amongst the children, as they cheered each other on and congratulated one another on their successes.
- It was clear that they were enjoying themselves, and I couldn't help but _____ at the sight.
- As the day wore on, the coaches introduced more complex drills and _____, pushing the children to test their limits and work together as a team.
- Even those who were initially hesitant or shy had loosened up and were fully participating, thanks to the _____ environment created by the coaches.

Read the story and circle whether the statement is true or false. If the statement is false, provide the correct answer for it.

The sports camp had no impact on the personal growth and development of the children.

True   False

The children participated in a variety of fun games and activities such as soccer, ball throwing and relay races.

True   False

The coaches were not doing a good job of keeping the children engaged.

True   False

The children worked together as a team and supported one another.

True   False

The little girl struggled with soccer drills all day and didn't eventually score a goal.

True   False

Read the story 'Sports camp' and answer the following questions.

What was the purpose of the sports camp organized by the school for third graders during the summer holidays?

What types of games and activities did the children participate in at the camp?

How did the coaches encourage the children to work together as a team?

Can you describe a moment from the story where a child overcame a challenge with the help of their teammates and coaches?

What life skills did the sports camp teach the children?

Assess your reading fluency by writing the number of words read per minute.

The school had organized a sports camp for the third graders during the summer holidays.	15
The idea was to keep the children physically active, while also giving them an opportunity to learn new skills and make new friends.	38
As I approached the field where the camp was being held, I could see dozens of children running around, laughing, and shouting with enthusiasm.	62
The coaches were doing an excellent job of keeping the children engaged, with a variety of fun games and activities.	82
There was a soccer station where the children were practicing their dribbling and shooting skills.	97
Another station had them throwing and catching balls with precision and accuracy.	109
Yet another station had them racing each other in relay races, their faces flushed with excitement.	125
I was impressed by the camaraderie amongst the children, as they cheered each other on and congratulated one another on their successes.	147
It was clear that they were enjoying themselves, and I couldn't help but smile at the sight.	164
As the day wore on, the coaches introduced more complex drills and exercises, pushing the children to test their limits and work together as a team.	190
Even those who were initially hesitant or shy had loosened up and were fully participating, thanks to the supportive environment created by the coaches.	214
I was particularly impressed by one little girl who had been struggling with the soccer drills earlier in the day.	237

With encouragement from her teammates and the coaches, she persisted and eventually scored a goal, much to the delight of everyone watching.	256
As the camp ended, the children gathered around the coaches for a group photo. They were sweaty and tired, but their faces were lit up with pride and accomplishment.	285
The coaches handed out certificates and medals, recognizing each child's unique contributions and achievements.	299
As I walked away from the camp, I couldn't help but feel grateful for the experience.	315
The sports camp had not only kept the children active and healthy but had also taught them valuable life skills such as teamwork, perseverance, and sportsmanship.	341
It was a wonderful example of how sports can be used as a tool for personal growth and development.	360

Date			
Words per minute			
Number of errors			

Make sentences using the words written below.

Sports
_____
_____

Games
_____
_____

Physical
_____
_____

discover
_____
_____

Coach
_____
_____

Activity
_____
_____

> Make a story using only five verbs from the following.

approached   running   laughing
shouting   engaged   practicing
throwing   catching   racing

> **Read the following story and underline all the adjectives. Use any five adjectives from the paragraph to write a story in your own words.**

Sports Day was a spectacular event, full of excitement and energy. The atmosphere was electric, with cheers and applause filling the air as competitors pushed themselves to the limit. The athletes were strong, agile, and determined, their muscles rippling with effort as they raced towards the finish line. The sun blazed down on the field, casting everything in a golden glow. It was a day of triumph and pride, as winners were crowned, and records were broken. The crowd was thrilled by the displays of skill and athleticism, and everyone left the stadium feeling exhilarated and inspired by what they had witnessed.

Story

Read the following story and underline all the conjunctions. Use any five conjunctions from the paragraph to write a story in your own words.

The baseball match was a real nail-biter as the two teams clashed in an epic battle. The stands were packed with fans who were eagerly anticipating the game, and the tension was palpable. The players were focused and determined, both eager to claim victory. The pitchers threw curveballs and fastballs, while the batters swung their bats with precision and power. The game was neck-and-neck, with each team scoring and then immediately conceding points. Eventually, in the ninth inning, the home team hit a walk-off homerun, and the stadium erupted with joy and relief. It was a thrilling game, filled with excitement and drama, and it left everyone feeling exhilarated and exhausted.

Story

Find and circle the words written below.

sports   camp   play
participate   enjoy   limits   test

h	e	x	p	l	o	r	e	k	f	y	d
a	t	p	e	n	j	o	y	k	s	j	l
e	a	f	i	m	k	k	w	j	a	m	i
s	p	h	l	i	m	p	i	n	w	e	m
f	i	r	e	g	t	e	n	v	n	m	i
y	c	a	i	n	t	c	g	l	b	n	t
l	i	d	p	b	r	u	s	h	s	c	s
y	t	p	z	i	n	g	s	t	a	z	c
a	r	m	j	l	u	j	e	c	s	b	s
l	a	a	o	r	f	u	e	g	t	e	a
p	p	c	o	s	p	o	r	t	s	t	t

Read the following paragraph and answer the questions asked below.

Sam was a happy boy who loved playing with his pet dog. They would run around the park together, chasing after sticks and balls. Sam's dog was his best friend, and he always made him laugh with his silly antics. Playing with his dog was Sam's favorite thing to do, and he felt so lucky to have him in his life.

Answer the questions asked below.

1. What is the name of the boy in the story?

_____

2. What kind of pet does Sam have?

_____

3. Where does Sam like to play with his dog?

_____

4. What is Sam's favorite thing to do with his dog?

_____

5. How does Sam feel about his pet dog?

_____

6. Give a title to the story.

_____

Read the following paragraph and choose the best answer to the questions asked below.

Marry adored her mermaid doll, a special gift from her grandma. She spent hours playing with it, imagining herself swimming in the ocean with her new friend. The doll's sparkling tail and flowing hair enchanted her, and Marry felt as if she had a real mermaid by her side.

Answer the questions asked below.

1. What is the name of the girl in the story?

a) Jane   b) Sarah   c) Marry   d) Lily

2. Who gave Marry the mermaid doll?

a) Her mom   b) Her dad   c) Her grandma   d) Her best friend

3. What did Marry imagine herself doing with the mermaid doll?

a) Playing with it in the park   b) Swimming in the ocean with her

c) Flying through the clouds   d) Riding a bicycle together

4. What was special about the mermaid doll's appearance?

a) It had wings   b) It had a sparkling tail and flowing hair

c) It glowed in the dark   d) It could talk

5. How did Marry feel about her new doll?

a) She didn't like it   b) She thought it was okay

c) She loved it   d) She was scared of it

6. What did Marry feel like when she played with the mermaid doll?

a) Happy and enchanted   b) Bored and uninterested

c) Anxious and scared   d) Angry and frustrated

Read the following paragraph and choose whether the statement is true or false.

Rufus, a friendly golden retriever, had an unlikely best friend named Whiskers, a curious little calico cat. Although their friendship was special, many of the other animals in the neighborhood judged Rufus for being friends with a cat. They thought it was strange and didn't understand how a dog and a cat could get along so well.

Despite the judgment, Rufus didn't care what others thought. He loved playing with Whiskers, chasing her through the grass and cuddling up with her on lazy afternoons. They were always there for each other, whether it was to share a meal or to comfort one another during thunderstorms.

Their friendship only grew stronger over time, and Rufus knew that Whiskers was the best friend he'd ever had. Even though others may not have understood their bond, it didn't matter to Rufus. All that mattered was the love and joy that came from spending time with his best friend, Whiskers.

Choose whether the statement is true or false.

1. Rufus is a cat.

True   False 0

2. Whiskers is a calico cat.

True   False

3. Many of the other animals in the neighborhood judged Rufus for being friends with a cat.

True   False

4. Rufus stopped being friends with Whiskers because of the judgment from other animals.

True   False

5. Rufus thought it was strange that he could be friends with a cat.

True   False

> **Read the following paragraph and fill in the blank spaces to complete the sentences.**

Emma is an ocean lover who goes on a snorkeling vacation with her family. As soon as she reaches the tropical destination, she can't wait to jump in the water and explore the underwater world. Emma spends every moment exploring the coral reefs, seeing schools of fish, sea urchins, starfish, and even a sea turtle. Over time, Emma learned to dive deeper and to hold her breath for extended periods. She became fascinated by the beauty and magic of the underwater world, and the experience left her breathless. Although the vacation came to an end, it was a journey that created lasting memories. Emma knew that the sea would always be a part of her, and she couldn't wait until the next time she could explore the underwater world once more.

Fill in the blank spaces.

1. Emma had always been drawn to the _____.
2. Emma's family decided to go on a _____ vacation.
3. As Emma dipped her head beneath the surface, a whole new world opened up before her _____.
4. Emma saw schools of _____ fish darting through the coral reefs.
5. She even caught a glimpse of a _____ turtle gliding gracefully through the water.
6. Over time, Emma learned to dive down deeper and how to hold her breath for longer _____ of time.
7. Although the vacation came to an end, it was a journey that created lasting _____.
8. Emma couldn't wait to put on her _____ gear and jump into the water.
9. Emma felt like she was part of a _____ world when she snorkeled.
10. Emma discovered more and more _____ she had never seen before during her snorkeling adventures.
11. Emma knew that the sea would always be a part of _____.
12. Although the vacation came to an end, Emma couldn't wait for the next time she could explore the _____ world again.

Read the following paragraph and answer the questions asked below.

Adam was fascinated by the space world. He dreamed of exploring the galaxies and traveled to the stars in his imagination. One night, he had a beautiful dream that took him on a journey through space in his own spaceship. It was a dream he would never forget.

Answer the questions asked below.

1. Who is the protagonist in the story?

_____

2. What was the setting for Adam's dream?

_____

3. What did Adam dream of doing in his imagination?

_____

4. What kind of vehicle did Adam use to travel through space in his dream?

_____

5. How did Adam feel when he woke up from his dream?

_____

6. Give a title to the story.

_____

Read the following paragraph and choose the best answer to the questions asked below.

Lena found a magical pen that could make anything she wrote come true. She was thrilled and wrote about things she always wanted to happen. Suddenly, everything started to change for the better. Her grades improved, she made new friends and her family grew closer. Lena knew that her magical pen was responsible for all the good things happening in her life.

Answer the questions asked below.

1. What kind of pen did Lena find?

a) A ballpoint pen b) A magical pen c) A fountain pen d) A gel pen

What happened when Lena wrote with the magic pen?

a) Her writing disappeared   b) Her writing became invisible

c) Whatever she wrote came true   d) Nothing happened

2. did Lena write with her magic pen?

a) A shopping list   b) A letter to her friend

c) A story   d) Things she wanted to happen

3. How did Lena's grades improve?

a) Because of studying hard   b) Because of the magic pen

c) Because of a new teacher   d) Because of her friends' help

4. What happened to Lena's family after she found the magic pen?

a) They moved away   b) They became closer

c) They started fighting   d) They stopped talking to each other

Read the following paragraph and choose whether the statement is true or false.

Princess Isabella was always sad and rarely smiled. The king and queen tried their best to make her happy, but nothing seemed to work. Then one day, a new nanny arrived at the palace. Her name was Maria, and she had a cheerful personality that lifted everyone's spirits. Maria spent time with Princess Isabella, playing games, telling stories, and teaching her new skills. Slowly but surely, the princess began to smile more and more. The king and queen were delighted to see their daughter happy again. They were grateful to Maria for bringing joy into their lives and making the palace a happier place.

Choose whether the statement is true or false.

1. Princess Isabella was always happy.

    True   False

2. The king and queen were upset when Maria arrived at the palace.

    True   False

3. A new nanny named Maria came to the palace.

    True   False

4. Maria had a sad personality that made everyone feel worse.

    True   False

5. Maria spent time with Princess Isabella playing games and telling stories.

    True   False

6. The king and queen tried to make their daughter happy.

    True   False

Read the following story and answer the questions asked below.

Daisy was a little yellow duck who loved to waddle around the pond. However, there was one thing that scared her, swimming. Every time her mother tried to teach her how to swim, Daisy would quack in fear and flap her wings about. Her mother didn't want to push her too hard, but she knew that swimming was important for ducks.

One day, a group of ducks came to the pond to swim. Daisy watched them from afar, envious of their graceful movements in the water. She longed to be like them but was too afraid. That's when a kind old turtle named Tim noticed her and asked her what was wrong. Daisy told him about her fear, and Tim offered to help her.

Over the next few days, Tim patiently taught Daisy how to swim. At first, she was hesitant, but as she practiced more and more, she grew more confident. Finally, the day arrived when Daisy took her first brave strokes across the pond. It wasn't easy, but with Tim's encouragement, she did it. Daisy was thrilled to realize that she could swim after all. From that day on, she happily joined the other ducks in the pond, feeling proud of herself and grateful to Tim.

Answer the questions asked below.

1. What was the name of the little duck that was afraid of swimming?

_____

_____

2. How did Daisy feel when her mother tried to teach her how to swim?

_____

_____

Answer the questions asked below.

3. How did Daisy feel when her mother tried to teach her how to swim?

_____

_____

4. What did a group of ducks do that made Daisy envious?

_____

_____

5. Who helped Daisy overcome her fear of swimming?

_____

_____

6. Why did Daisy's mother think swimming was important for ducks?

_____

_____

7. How did Tim help Daisy to overcome her fear of swimming?

_____

_____

Made in the USA
Coppell, TX
26 February 2025